*With thanks to God,
who promises to give His children
all the light they need
to find their way
through every maze of life.*

Acknowledgments

With special thanks to some unsung heroes at Harvest House Publishers who make sure every book is the best it can be before it goes to press. There's a lot of work involved in getting a book ready for the printing process, and the people in the Production Department—Dallas Richards, Jennifer Hass, Gary Lineburg, Ty Pauls, and Corey Fisher—are the ones who make it happen. Thanks for helping to get this book printed and into the hands of children (and adults!) who will enjoy it.

And with affectionate appreciation to our sons Keith, Nathan, and Ryan, who for many nights looked over our shoulders with great interest as we created this book. They gave us some great ideas that appear in these mazes!

Welcome to Amazing Mazes!

We're glad you're joining us for some exciting adventures through the many wonderful stories in the Bible. We'll start at the same place the Bible begins—in the book of Genesis, where we read about how God created the universe. From there, we'll go on to meet Noah, Moses, Ruth, David, Daniel, Mary, and many other people who were friends with God. Most important of all, we'll get to meet Jesus, learn why He came to earth, and discover how much He loves us.

Each maze in this book comes with a story you'll want to read. And under the title of each story we've given the Bible chapters and verses where you will find that same story in your Bible.

Come join us . . . and learn more about our amazing God and what He has done for His children!

Steve & Becky Miller

The Old Testament

The Old Testament

Here are the names of the books in the Old Testament of the Bible. However, the letters are all mixed up! Can you spell the names of the books correctly?

neGises	slcEciastees
dxsouE	ngoS fo Snsgo
tevicLsui	isIhaa
srebmNu	rmeeihJa
ymoteuDeron	ttionamesnLa
uahsoJ	liezkEe
Jgedsu	aDniel
hRtu	eoasH
1 meluaS	lJeo
2 lSeuam	osmA
1 ginsK	hadiabO
2 iKgns	aoJhn
1 hroncleCis	hciaM
2 nhrlesoCci	Nahmu
rzaE	kHkabaku
eehmiahN	iahZehpan
rEtshe	gaiagH
obJ	hiarchZae
samlPs	aMachli
vbroPrse	

AMAZING MAZES for KIDS

STEVE & BECKY MILLER

HARVEST HOUSE PUBLISHERS
Eugene, Oregon 97402

The authors may be reached at
P.O. Box 1011, Springfield, OR 97478
or e-mailed at
srmbook123@aol.com

AMAZING MAZES FOR KIDS

Copyright © 1998 by Steve & Becky Miller
Published by Harvest House Publishers
Eugene, Oregon 97402

ISBN 1-56507-846-2

98 99 00 01 02 03 / BP / 10 9 8 7 6 5 4 3 2 1

Use this page to spell the book names correctly. If you need help, you can use your Bible.

_____	_____
_____	_____
_____	_____
_____	_____
_____	_____
_____	_____
_____	_____
_____	_____
_____	_____
_____	_____
_____	_____
_____	_____
_____	_____
_____	_____
_____	_____
_____	_____
_____	_____
_____	_____
_____	_____

(The answers are on page 154 in the back of the book.)

In the Beginning,
God Spoke . . .

Genesis 1-2

Where did our world come from—the earth, sun, moon, stars, and universe?

God made everything. It all began long ago when He spoke, saying, "Let there be light." And there was light! Then God spoke again, and made the sky, land, seas, animals, and plants. Last, He made Adam and Eve. All this happened when God spoke words! Isn't God an amazing artist?

Can you find your way through the letters in the maze and get to the earth? When you're done, color in the letters that have black dots. What do they spell?

FINISH

God Creates
Man and Woman

Genesis 2:18-22

After God created all the animals, He made a man and
named him Adam. When Adam walked through the
Garden of Eden, he saw that every animal had a friend of
the same kind. But Adam was alone. God knew Adam
needed a friend—a special kind of friend. While Adam

was sleeping, God made a woman. Her name was Eve. Together they enjoyed the beautiful garden God had made for them.

Can you help Adam find Eve?

Adam and Eve Disobey God

Genesis 3

God gave Adam and Eve a wonderful place to live—the Garden of Eden. The garden was filled with beautiful plants, trees, and animals.

God told Adam and Eve to enjoy the garden, but He gave them one warning: "Do not eat the fruit on the tree of the knowledge of good and evil, or you will die."

One day a snake came to Eve and said, "Look at how pretty the fruit is! Doesn't it look delicious? If you eat it, you will become as wise as God."

Eve thought the fruit looked good and picked one. She took a bite, then gave some to Adam.

Suddenly they realized something was wrong. They had done something God told them not to do!

God called them. "Where are you?" He asked. Adam and Eve tried to hide because they knew they had disobeyed God. "Because you have eaten the fruit, you must leave the garden," said God.

Adam and Eve left the garden, and God sent angels with fiery swords to prevent anyone from ever entering the garden again.

Can you start at the tree root and find your way to the fruit Eve is about to pick?

START

Noah Builds an Ark

Genesis 6-7

More and more people were born on the earth, and many of them chose to disobey God and do wicked things. This made God sad. The only righteous people He could find were Noah and his wife. God told Noah, "I am going to bring a flood to wipe away all the people on the earth. I want you to build an ark for your family and two of every kind of living creature. You are also to take every kind of food to help feed yourselves and the animals while you are on the ark."

Noah obeyed God and built the ark. Do you know how long it took for him to build it? One hundred and twenty years!

While Noah built the ark, he told people about God's warning. But no one listened to him. They did not believe that God would destroy everything on the earth.

On the next page, do you see the little mouse next to Noah? Can you help the mouse find his friend at the top of the ark?

The Big Flood
Genesis 7-8

When Noah finished building the ark, he gathered his family and every kind of animal into the ark with him. After that, just as God promised, great rains came upon the earth for 40 days and 40 nights. The floodwaters grew higher and higher, until even the highest mountains on the earth were completely covered.

Can you help the animals find their way to the ark?

The Rain Stops
Genesis 7-8

After the rain stopped and the water began to go down, the ark came to rest on a mountain. Noah sent a dove out to find some dry land. But the floodwaters were still too high, and the dove returned to the ark.

Seven days later, Noah sent the dove out again. This time, when the dove returned, there was an olive leaf in its beak!

Can you help the bird near the ark find the olive plant at the end of the maze?

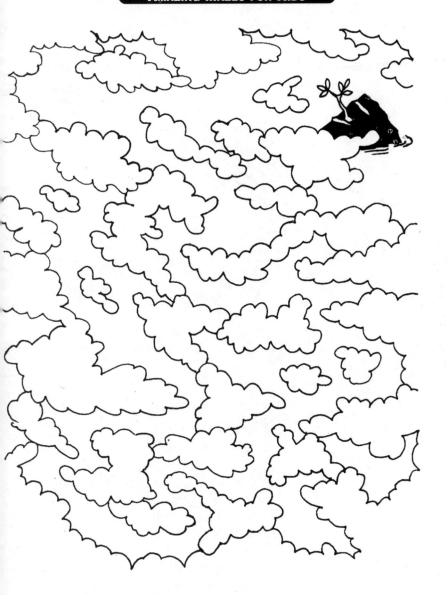

The First Rainbow
Genesis 9

When God told Noah, "Come out of the ark," everyone was excited to be free again! Noah wanted to give thanks to God for protecting him and his family, so he built an alter and gave a burnt offering to the Lord.

God then told Noah, "Never again will I destroy the earth with a flood. To remind you of My promise, I will place a rainbow in the sky."

Can you find your way from the beginning of the rainbow over to the ark? When you are done, color the rainbow!

God's Promise to Abraham and Sarah

Genesis 12, 18, 21

Abraham and Sarah lived in a place called Ur. One day God told Abraham, "I am going to give you many children, and they will become a great nation. I want you to go to a new land where your people will live someday."

Abraham and Sarah left their home, and traveled to the new land. Many years went by, but they had no children. Again, God told Abraham, "I will give you a son."

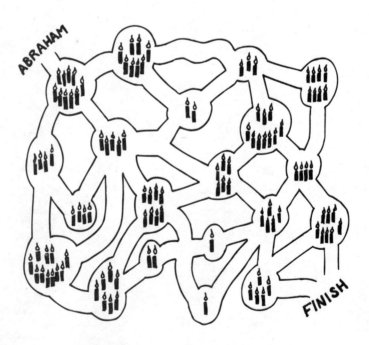

But more years went by, and still they had no son. They became very old and began to think it was impossible for them to have a child.

Finally, when Abraham was 100 years old, and Sarah was 90, God gave them a son. They named him Isaac and were very happy because God had kept His promise!

There are two mazes below—one for Abraham, and one for Sarah. Can you figure out how to go through Abraham's maze and gather exactly 100 birthday candles? Now go through Sarah's maze and gather exactly 90 birthday candles.

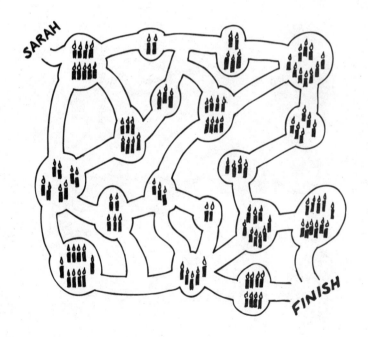

A Wife for Isaac
Genesis 24

When Isaac was ready to become married, his father, Abraham, wanted to help him find a godly wife. Abraham called one of his servants and asked him to travel back to his homeland to find a wife for Isaac.

The servant took ten camels for the journey. When he arrived at his destination, he prayed and asked God to

help him find the right woman. At the end of his prayer, a lovely woman named Rebekah came up and offered to give water to the camels. The servant knew this was the right woman and took her back to the land where Abraham and Isaac lived. She became a wonderful wife for Isaac.

The ropes for the camels have gotten all mixed up. Can you find out which rope belongs to which camel?

The Birthright Stew

Genesis 25:19-34

Isaac and Rebekah gave birth to twin boys, Jacob and Esau. The boys were very different. Esau was born first and was red and hairy. He became a skilled hunter. Jacob did not look like Esau, and was a quiet man who worked around the family tents.

One day, Jacob was cooking some stew. Esau had just finished a long, hard hunting trip and smelled the good stew. He said, "Hurry, give me that stew! I'm starving!"

But Jacob said, "First, sell me your birthright."

Esau agreed to sell his birthright, trading it for Jacob's stew. When Esau was finished eating, he got up and left.

What had Esau done? Remember, Esau was the firstborn child. Back in those days, the firstborn child received the biggest inheritance after his parents died. This was called a "birthright." Because Esau was born first, he had the birthright. But when he arrived home from his hunting trip, he traded his birthright for Jacob's stew. That meant Jacob now had the birthright. When their parents died, Jacob would get the biggest inheritance, not Esau.

Esau did not take good care of his birthright, and Jacob had tricked his brother into giving up the birthright.

Can you find your way through the steam and get to the bowl of stew?

Jacob and Rachel

Genesis 29:16-30

After Jacob took Esau's birthright, there were more problems between the brothers. Jacob was afraid Esau would kill him, so he traveled far away to the home of his Uncle Laban.

When he arrived, he met a beautiful woman named Rachel. She was the daughter of Laban, and took care of the family sheep.

Jacob asked his Uncle Laban if he could marry Rachel. The uncle said, "First, you must work for me for seven years." Jacob loved Rachel so much, he was willing to work hard to marry her.

Can you help Jacob find his way to Rachel?

Joseph,
the Favorite Son
Genesis 37

Jacob had 12 sons. One of the sons, Joseph, was his favorite. He loved Joseph so much that he gave him a beautiful coat of many colors.

Joseph's brothers did not like all the attention their father gave to Joseph. They were angry against Joseph, but did not know what to do.

One day Jacob said to Joseph, "Your brothers have gone away to another place to graze the sheep. They have been gone for a while. Can you go to your brothers and make sure all is well with them?"

Joseph traveled through the countryside to find his brothers. They saw him in the distance and said, "There is Joseph! What shall we do to him?"

The brothers agreed to take Joseph's coat away and throw him into an empty well. A little later, some traders passed by on their way to Egypt. The brothers wanted to get rid of Joseph, so they sold him to the traders. This meant Joseph would be taken to Egypt to become a slave.

When the brothers returned home, they lied to their father and told him that Joseph had been eaten by a wild animal.

Can you find your way through Joseph's colored coat? When you are finished, color the coat.

Joseph Goes
to Egypt
Genesis 39:1-6

Joseph and his brothers lived in the land of Canaan, the land where the nation of Israel is today. When his brothers sold him into slavery, Joseph was taken to Egypt. It was a long journey, which meant Joseph would be far away from home. He did not know if he would ever see his family again.

Can you find the route that the slave traders will use to take Joseph to Egypt?

START

The Pharaoh's Dream
Genesis 41

Joseph was all alone in Egypt, but God took care of him. There was a special reason God had allowed Joseph to be taken to Egypt.

One night, the king of the Egyptians—the Pharaoh—had a dream. In the dream he saw seven fat, healthy cows. Then he saw seven sick, starving cows.

Then the Pharaoh had a second dream. He saw seven healthy heads of grain growing on a single stalk. Then he saw seven thin, dry heads of grain.

In the morning, the Pharaoh could not forget about the strange dreams. He called all his magicians and the wise men of Egypt, but no one could interpret the dreams.

One man said, "I know someone who can help interpret your dream. His name is Joseph."

When Joseph came before the king, the Pharaoh asked, "Can you interpret my dream?"

"I cannot," said Joseph, "but God will give you the answer."

After Pharaoh described the dream, Joseph said, "God is telling you that for seven years Egypt will have much food. But after those seven years are over, there will be seven years of famine, and there will be no food. This means you must start saving as much food as possible so we will have enough to make it through the famine."

The Pharaoh saw that Joseph was wise, and he made Joseph a ruler over all of Egypt!

Can you find your way through the field of grain and get to the grain-filled pots at the end?

The Hebrews Become Slaves

Exodus 1

After Joseph became ruler over Egypt, his family left the land of Canaan and moved to Egypt. Everyone was happy to be back together again. Joseph's people, also known as the children of Israel, did well in Egypt.

Many years later, after Joseph died, there was a new Pharaoh in Egypt. He had forgotten about Joseph's good deeds. He was afraid of the Israelites because there were so many of them. So he made them into slaves, forcing them to work hard and make bricks.

Can you find your way through the bricks and get to the palm tree?

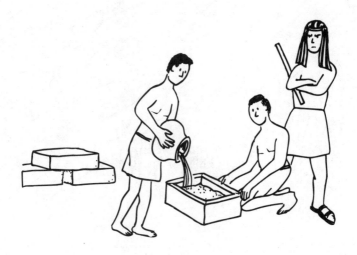

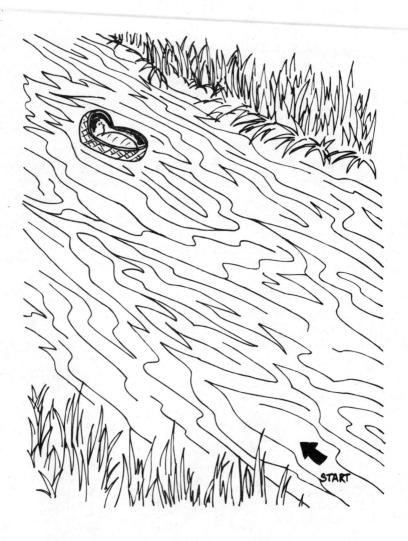

START

The Baby in a Basket
Exodus 1:1-2:10

The new Pharaoh was a wicked king. When he made the Israelites into slaves, he made a new rule: "If an Israelite family gives birth to a baby boy, the baby must be thrown into the Nile River. Only baby girls can live."

One Israelite mother did not want to hurt her baby boy. At first she hid him so he would not be found. But when he was three months old, he had become too big and noisy to hide.

The mother decided to make a basket and cover it with tar and pitch. Then she put her baby in the basket, and let it float on the river. The baby boy's sister quietly hid herself in the reeds along the riverbank. She wanted to see what would happen to him.

Just then the Pharaoh's daughter went to the river and saw the baby in the basket. He was crying, and she felt sorry for him.

When the Pharaoh's daughter picked up the baby, the boy's sister came up and asked, "Would you like me to get an Israelite mother to nurse him for you?"

"Yes," said the Pharaoh's daughter.

Guess which mother the sister got? Their own mother! So the baby's mother was allowed to take care of Moses until he was old enough to live with the Pharaoh's daughter.

Starting from the arrow in the reeds, can you find your way to Moses' basket?

START

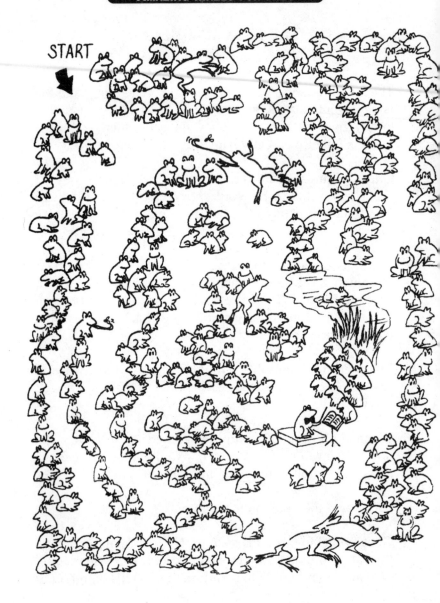

The Ten Plagues
Exodus 5-12

Moses grew up in the Pharaoh's house, but in his heart he knew he was an Israelite. He wished he could help free his people from slavery. One time when he tried to help the Israelites, he got in trouble, so he ran away.

Forty years later, God told Moses to go back and ask the Pharaoh to free the Israelites. But the Pharaoh refused to let the people go. Then God warned, "I will send ten terrible plagues on Egypt!"

In one of the plagues, God sent frogs all over Egypt. Can you find your way through the frogs?

The Miracle at the Red Sea
Exodus 12:31-15:21

After the last plague, the Pharaoh told Moses, "Take your people away!" At last, the Israelites were free! They left Egypt quickly.

But then the Pharaoh changed his mind and sent his army after the Israelites, who were now at the Red Sea.

When the Israelites saw the army chasing them, they became afraid. But God told them not to worry. A strong wind blew, and the Red Sea parted. The Israelites were able to escape! After everyone got to the other side, the sea crashed down, killing all the Egyptian soldiers.

Can you find your way to the priests who are carrying the Ark of the Covenant at the front of the crowd?

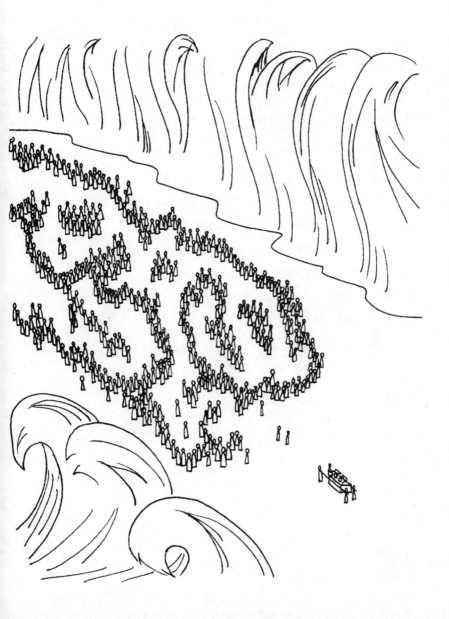

The Ten Commandents

Exodus 20:1-17

God wanted to help prepare His people for living in their new land. He wanted them to understand the difference between right and wrong. So He gave them His law, the Ten Commandments, which were given to Moses on two tablets of stone. Can you unscramble the words in the Ten Commandments? Use the blank lines on the next page.

1. me before gods any have Do other not

2. yourselves not Do make idols for

3. name Do vain take Lord the not of the in

4. day keep to Remember Sabbath the

5. mother father your and Honor

6. not anyone murder Do

7. commit not adultery Do

8. not Do steal

9. lie Do not

10. covet people's other not things Do

In Luke 10:27, Jesus said the whole law could be described in just two commands:

- Love God with all your heart, soul, mind, and strength.

- Love other people just like you love yourself.

Insert the unscrambled words of the Ten Commandments on the lines below.

1. _____

2. _____

3. _____

4. _____

5. _____

6. _____

7. _____

8. _____

9. _____

10. _____

Afraid of the Giants

Numbers 13-14

When the Israelites arrived at the edge of the Promised Land, God told Moses, "Send some men to explore the land which I am giving to you." Twelve men were chosen to check the land. The rest of the people set up camp and waited until the twelve explorers came back.

When the men returned, ten of them said, "This land is wonderful! We brought back some grapes which are so big we needed two men to carry them! But the people who live in that land are giants, and their cities have strong, thick walls. They will destroy us!"

However, two of the explorers, Joshua and Caleb, said, "It is true that the land is good. But we should not be afraid to enter it, because God is with us. He promised to give us the land!"

The people did not listen to Joshua and Caleb. They became afraid, and wanted to go back to Egypt.

God was angry at the Israelites for being afraid. "Because you do not believe Me, you will not go into the land. You will wander in the wilderness for 40 years."

The cluster of grapes that the explorers brought back from the Promised Land was very large. Can you find your way through the cluster?

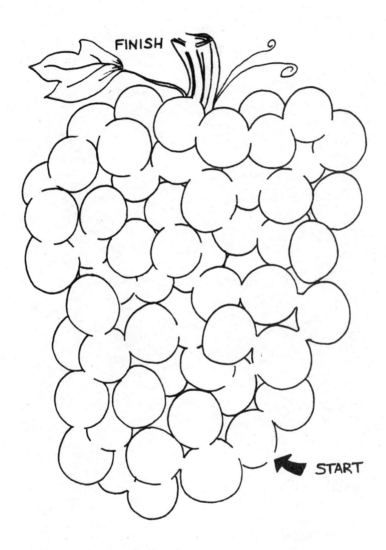

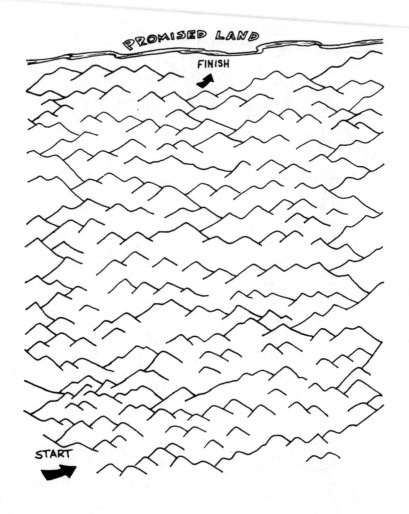

The 40-Year Journey
Numbers 15-34

Just as God promised, the Israelites had to wander in the wilderness for 40 years. During those years, many new Israelite children were born, and the older people who had not trusted God died. By the time Israel's 40-year journey came to an end, all the people had been replaced. Only Joshua and Caleb were allowed to survive because they had trusted God.

Can you find your way through the wilderness to the edge of the Promised Land?

Marching Around Jericho

Joshua 1-6

When the Israelites came back to the Promised Land, Moses died, and Joshua became their new leader. He sent two spies into the land and told them to look carefully at Jericho.

When the spies came back, Joshua told the Israelites, "God will give us the land. He wants us to destroy the wicked people; He will help us."

The first city they went to was Jericho, which had tall, strong walls. How were they to conquer the city?

God told the people to march around Jericho one time each day for six days. Then, on the seventh day, they were to march around Jericho seven times, blow their trumpets, and shout.

When the seventh day arrived, the people followed God's instructions, and the walls came tumbling down! Now the Israelites knew that God would help them conquer the Promised Land.

Can you help the Israelites find their way around Jericho and get to the front gates?

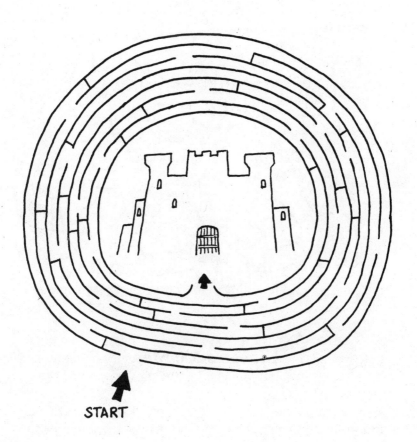

START

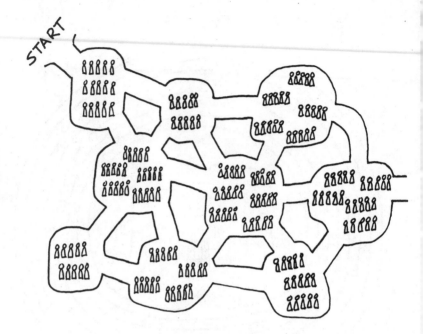

Gideon's 300 Men

Judges 6-7

After Joshua died, the people of Israel forgot about God and sinned against Him. So God sent some enemies to hurt the Israelites and take their land away.

The Israelites became afraid and prayed to God. "Please help us!" they cried.

God chose a man named Gideon to bring together an army to get rid of Israel's enemies. Gideon gathered thousands of men for his army, but God said that was too many. "Take the men to some water and watch how they drink. Only those who use their hands to bring water to their lips are to help with the battle."

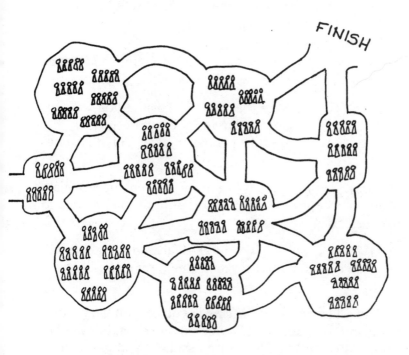

After that, Gideon had only 300 men left. How could 300 men possibly beat the huge enemy army? But God was with the Israelites! When Gideon and his men snuck up on the enemy camp with their torches and trumpets, the enemy soldiers became so frightened they ran away! Once again, God protected the people of Israel and kept them safe.

Can you go through the maze and help Gideon find exactly 300 men?

The Strongest Man in Israel
Judges 13-16

When Samson was born, God told his mother and father, "Samson must never cut his hair, or he will lose his strength."

Samson was so strong that he once killed a lion with his bare hands. His great strength brought fear to the Philistines, who hated the people of Israel. The Philistines wanted to kill Samson.

One day Samson met a beautiful woman named Delilah. She was a Philistine, but Samson did not care. He loved her very much.

The Philistines secretly went to Delilah and said, "We will give you a lot of money if you tell us what makes Samson so strong."

Delilah asked Samson, "Where do you get your strength?" For many days, Samson did not tell his secret. But Delilah kept asking, and finally Samson said, "If you really must know, I can never cut my hair, or I will become weak."

Delilah then told the Philistines Samson's secret. Later, while Samson was asleep, the Philistines sneaked up on him and shaved off his hair. When he woke up, he tried to fight, but his strength was gone.

The Philistines blinded Samson and made him work hard grinding grain. Then one day when they were having a feast, they said, "Bring out Samson so we can laugh at him!" When Samson was brought out, he asked God, "Please help me to take revenge on the Philistines!" Then he put his hands on two pillars and pushed. The whole building came crashing down, killing all the Philistines, and Samson with them.

Can you find your way through Samson's hair?

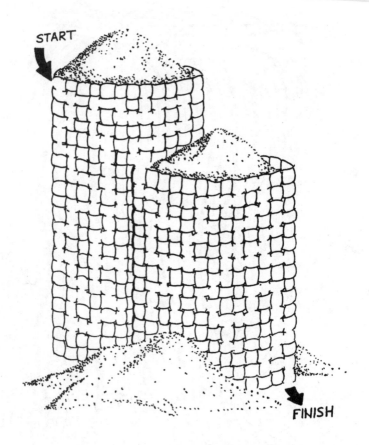

Ruth: A Faithful Daughter-in-Law

Ruth

Naomi grew up in Israel, but after she became married, she and her husband moved to Moab. They had two sons. One son married a woman named Orpah, and the other son married a woman named Ruth.

Later, Naomi's husband died, and her sons died, too. When Naomi told her two daughters-in-law that she was going back to Israel, Ruth said, "I will go with you!"

Naomi and Ruth arrived in Israel at harvest time. Because they had no food, Ruth said she would go gather grain that the workers had left in one of the fields.

Boaz, the owner of the field, noticed Ruth working hard. He made sure Ruth got plenty of grain. When Ruth brought the grain home, Naomi was surprised. Naomi said, "Boaz took good care of you!"

Boaz continued to show kindness to Ruth. Later they got married and had a little boy. The boy's name was Obed; this boy was to become the grandfather of David, who would be a great king in Israel.

Noami was glad she had come back to Israel. New she had a wonderful grandson, and Ruth had found a good husband and home!

See if you can find your way through the grain baskets.

START

FINISH

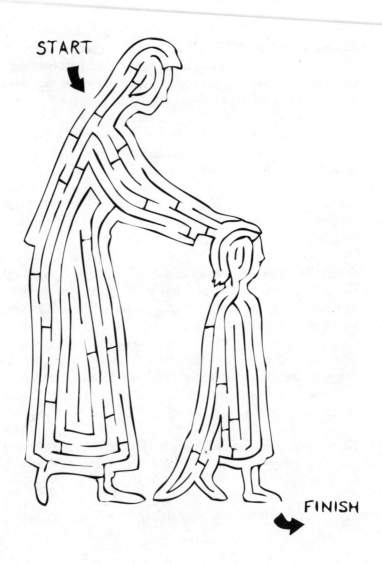

Hannah Gives Her
Child to God

1 Samuel 1:1-2:11

Hannah was sad because she had no children. She had a good husband who loved her, but still she cried because she wanted a child.

Every year, Hannah and her husband went to the tabernacle to worship God. During one of their visits, Hannah prayed, "Lord, please give me a son, and I will give him back to You to serve You all the days of his life."

God heard Hannah's prayer, and gave her a son. She named him Samuel because she had asked God for him.

Hannah was a good mother and taught Samuel about God. She prepared him for serving in the tabernacle. When he was old enough, she took Samuel to the priest at the tabernacle and said, "I prayed for this child, and God gave him to me. I promised I would give the child back to the Lord, and now I give him to serve God all of his life."

Samuel grew up and served God in the tabernacle and became a wise leader who did many great things for the nation of Israel.

Can you find your way through the maze?

Job—Faithful to God
Job

Long ago there was a man named Job who loved God very much. Job was a wise man, and had thousands of sheep and camels, and hundreds of oxen and donkeys. He also had seven sons and three daughters.

One day when the angels were standing before God, Satan came and stood with them. Satan told God, "Job loves you because You are so good to him. If Job were to lose everything he has, then he would turn away from You."

Later, Job lost all of his animals and all of his children. Job also became very sick with horrible sores all over his body. Job's wife became angry with God and tried to get Job mad at God. But Job did not. He still loved God.

When Job's friends heard about what had happened, they came to visit him. They thought that maybe God was punishing him. They said, "You have lost everything, and you are covered with sores. Surely you have done something wrong, and God is punishing you."

But Job said he had not sinned against God. He continued to trust God and stay faithful to Him.

Because Job was faithful, God made him well again. God also gave Job twice as many animals as he had had before! And once again, Job had seven sons and three daughters.

When Job was hurt and suffering, he did not become angry with God. He continued to love God. When we are suffering, we should follow Job's example. When we show God our love and stay close to Him, we allow Him to help us through our troubles.

```
J A J C D N J Q G C Y J N I S Z T A
I O O W R U O E J O B V O A M C J C
V Y B K M L B R A H Z G F B T K O Y
D O N Z W R T U L N J O B X C F B W
J Q V A J O B G H D O Q P T N O C G
K H C U W H U Y T K B F N V J W Z A
P G F J A I W Z M Q U L K F A O Y C
T Z C O M A V E J U J O B R W H B I
J D Q B Y N T H O P N T X C F E G L
R O S T L E J O B G M B D J P J O B
H W B Y V W Z M L P O U T O D C K L
P Y E S J B F W E J I D H B F Z M W
J O B Y R W J S C B O M Y H J O B G
D S A L M J O B P U Y B E Q V A T S
R J Y T E Q B M R S T L N E C D P R
K O D J C A Z W T M C Y S R M J K T
C B K X O P K C J O B M C K D Q O L
F R N Q M B Y V P Z N Q J O B N E B
```

How many times can you find the name *Job* in the above word search?

(The answers are on page 155 in the back of the book.)

Israel's First King
1 Samuel 8-10

Israel was ruled by God, but the other nations were ruled by human kings.

Israel wanted to be like the other nations, so the people went to Samuel and said, "We want a king like the other nations have."

Samuel was not happy. "God is your King," he said. But the people would not listen.

God told Samuel, "Go ahead; give them a king. But warn the people that a human king will make life harder for them."

In another place in Israel, a man named Kish lost his donkeys. Kish had a tall, handsome son named Saul. He said to Saul, "Our donkeys are lost. Go look for them, and bring them back."

Saul and a servant searched for three days, but could not find the donkeys. When they heard that Samuel was nearby, Saul said, "Maybe Samuel can tell us where the donkeys are."

When Saul came up to Samuel, Samuel said, "The donkeys have already been found." Then Samuel poured some oil on Saul's head and said, "God has chosen you to become the first king of Israel." Saul was very surprised! Now the people of Israel were happy because they had their own king.

Can you find your way through the crown?

START   FINISH

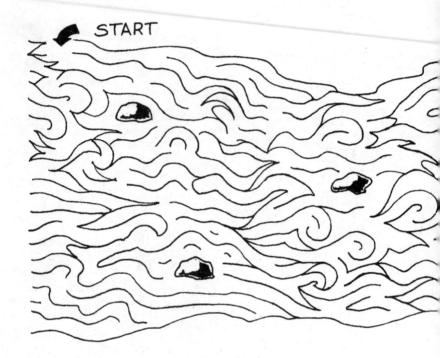

START

Five Smooth Stones
1 Samuel 17

David was a young shepherd boy who watched his father's sheep. One day, his father sent him to take food to his brothers, who were in Israel's army.

When David arrived at the army camp, he looked across the river and saw the enemy soldiers, the Philistines. A large, strong soldier named Goliath shouted, "Come fight me!" But the Israelites were afraid, and ran away.

FINISH

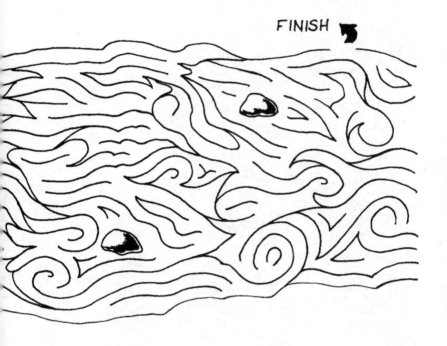

David saw Goliath and was not afraid. "I will fight Goliath!" he said. David went to a stream and got five smooth stones. He shouted to Goliath, "You have your sword and spear, but I have God!" David then slung a stone at Goliath's forehead, and the giant fell dead!

Can you help David find all five stones in the stream?

START

David Flees from Saul
1 Samuel 21-31

Saul was Israel's first king, but he did not follow God's commands. This made God sad. He knew He would have to pick another king to lead the nation of Israel.

God picked David, a young shepherd boy, to be the next king. Many people liked David, and David was good at everything he did. This made Saul jealous and angry. He tried to kill David, but David escaped. David ran away to the hills and rocks, and hid in a cave.

Saul tried to chase David but did not catch him. David stayed away from Jerusalem until Saul died. After Saul's death, David was able to return to Jerusalem and become Israel's new king.

Can you find your way across the hills and rocks to David's hiding place in the cave?

The Psalms—Songs to the Lord
Psalms

The book of Psalms is filled with special songs to the Lord. King David wrote many of the songs. When David and other Israelites sang these songs, they used different kinds of musical instruments, such as trumpets, bells, rams' horns, lutes, lyres, harps, cymbals, tambourines, flutes, and pipes. You'll find all of these instruments pictured here in the maze.

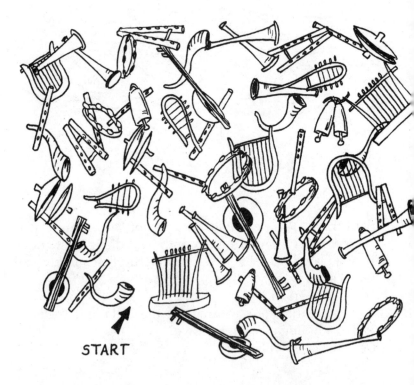

START

Can you find your way through the maze from beginning to end?

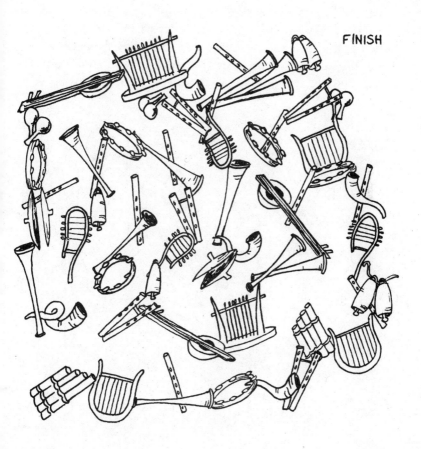

FINISH

Growing Strong in the Lord
Psalm 1:1-3

Psalm 1:1-3 tells us what happens when we love and obey God's Word, the Bible. In those verses we read, "Blessed is the man . . . [whose] delight is in the law of the LORD, and on his law he meditates day and night. He is like a tree planted by streams of water, which yields its fruit in season and whose leaf does not wither. Whatever he does prospers."

When a tree is next to a stream, it can drink all the water it needs so that its leaves stay green and it can bear fruit. In the same way, when we feed ourselves from the Bible— which is the same as listening to it and obeying it—then we will grow into strong Christians.Can you find your way to the big, strong tree next to the stream?

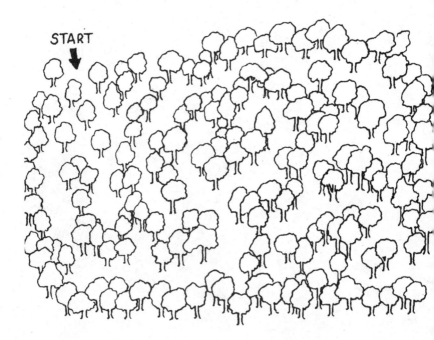

FINISH

The Wisest Man Who Ever Lived
2 Chronicles 1

After King David died, Solomon became the next king of Israel. One night, God spoke to Solomon and said, "Ask for whatever you want Me to give you." Solomon answered, "Please give me wisdom and knowledge so that I will know how to lead Your people."

God was pleased that Solomon asked for wisdom, and not riches or fame. He told Solomon, "Because you asked for wisdom, I will also give you great wealth and honor. You will be Israel's greatest king."

Solomon became very famous because of his wisdom, and he was so rich he had 1,400 chariots! Can you help Solomon find his way to the chariot that's ready for him at the end of the maze?

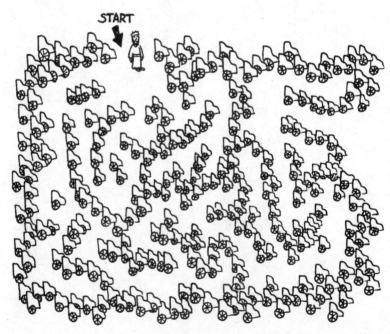

START

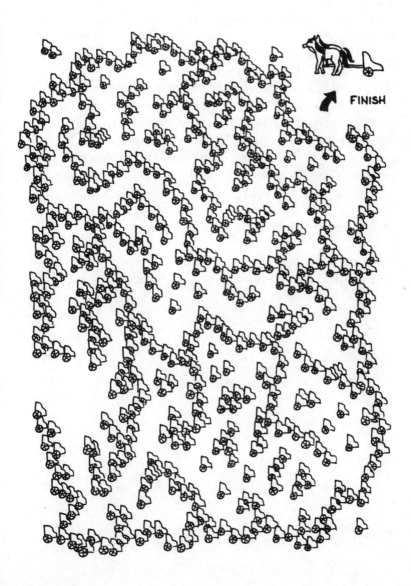

FINISH

Elijah and the Ravens
1 Kings 17:1-6

When King Solomon died, the nation of Israel divided into two parts—the Northern Kingdom and the Southern Kingdom. Most of the kings who ruled during that time did not follow God. They were wicked and turned the people of Israel against God.

This made God sad. He spoke to a prophet named Elijah, saying, "Because my people have turned away from Me, it will not rain in Israel for three years." Then God told Elijah, "You are to go to a brook east of the Jordan River. There, you will have water. I will also send ravens to bring bread and meat to you in the morning and the evening."

Just as God promised, when Elijah went to the brook, God sent ravens, or birds, with food for Elijah.

In the maze, can you help the raven at the top of the page get to Elijah, who is sitting next to the river?

God's Great Love
Lamentations 3:22-23

Do you know how much God loves His children, including you?

The prophet Jeremiah, who wrote the book of Lamentations, wrote these words: "The Lord's love never ends. His mercies never stop. They are new every morning" (Lamentations 3:22-23 ICB).

God's love for us is new every morning. His love never runs out—isn't that amazing? He is always ready to take care of our needs every day of our lives!

The words in Lamentations 3:22-23 are hidden in the word search on the next page. Can you find them?

```
M R S B D M T B N R S L T E
D O C A R G H I S Q D H R V
G L R U Z M E L R E M C A E
Q D H N O C G D C N E V E R
A M C X I P W A Q D Z S O Y
R G R B L N L U C S M R L A
E L M H F C G A B F T G B S
M Q E L R T L N E L O V E W
L O R D S G X D S U G H C B
D T C M U N B R M C S T O P
P R I C P D E C Z H R H X D
R Z E G C B H V G L D E G H
D G S L M R G D E X P Y C U
M C B A N E W O C R H W L R
```

THE	HIS	THEY
LORD'S	MERCIES	ARE
LOVE	NEVER	NEW
NEVER	STOP	EVERY
ENDS		MORNING

(The answers are on page 156 in the back of the book.)

Nebuchadnezzar's Giant Statue
Daniel 3

Long after King David and Solomon died, the people of Israel had become so wicked God warned they would be taken into captivity by their enemies. However, the Israelites did not listen to God. So the Lord sent the Babylonian army to Israel, and many of the Israelites were taken back to Babylon to become servants and slaves. Daniel and his three friends, Shadrach, Meshach, and Abednego, were all taken to Babylon.

King Nebuchadnezzar of Babylon decided to build a giant statue made of gold. He then asked all the people to bow down and worship it. Everyone bowed down before the statue, but Daniel's three friends did not. King Nebuchadnezzar became angry, and had the three friends thrown into a hot, fiery furnace.

But God protected Shadrach, Meshach, and Abednego. When Nebuchadnezzar saw that the three young men were not burned, he set them free and said, "The God of Israel is the greatest God of all!"

Can you find your way through the crowd of bowing people to get to the three friends?

FINISH

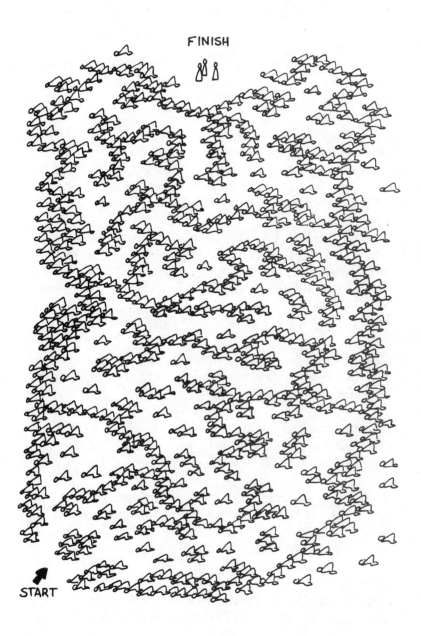

START

Daniel in the Lions' Den
Daniel 6

Daniel was so wise that the king of Babylon made Daniel into a powerful ruler. Some of the Babylonian leaders who helped the king did not like that.

The angry Babylonian leaders wanted to get rid of Daniel, and tried to find a way to get him into trouble. Daniel, however, was an honest, righteous man. They could not find anything wrong with him. Three times a day every day, Daniel prayed to God. He was a faithful man.

Finally Daniel's enemies came up with a wicked idea. They said, "Let's make a new law. Everyone in Babylon must worship our king, and no one else. Anyone who breaks the law will be thrown into the lions' den. Then if we catch Daniel praying to his God, he will be breaking the law, and we can put him to death."

After Daniel heard about the new law, he did not stop praying to God. He was not afraid of the horrible trap his enemies had set up for him.

The men arrested Daniel and had him thrown into the lions' den. The king of Babylon, who loved Daniel, did not want to punish him. But he knew he had to obey the new law.

That night, the king could not eat or sleep. He was concerned about Daniel. Very early the next morning, he got up and quickly went to the lions' den. He was overjoyed when he saw that Daniel was still alive!

"My God sent His angel, who shut the mouths of the lions," said Daniel. "They have not hurt me because I have done nothing wrong against God. Neither have I done anything wrong to you, O king."

The king became angry against Daniel's enemies and had them thrown into the lions' den. All of them were eaten by the lions. Then the king said, "Everyone in Babylon must worship the God of Daniel!"

Can you find your way through the maze in the lion's mane?

Esther: The Queen Who Saved Israel
Esther

When King Xerxes of Persia needed a new queen, he chose a young woman named Esther. He did not know it, but Esther was one of the Israelites. At that time, many Israelites lived as servants and slaves in Persia. Esther's uncle, whose name was Mordecai, told her, "Don't tell anyone you are from the land of Israel."

King Xerxes had many important officials in his royal court. One was a man named Haman. He hated Mordecai.

Haman wanted to get rid of Mordecai. He knew Mordecai was an Israelite, so he asked King Xerxes to make a new law: All the people of Israel were to be put to death! Because the king did not know Queen Esther was an Israelite, he didn't realize she would have to die, too.

When Mordecai heard about the new rule, he told Esther, "King Xerxes plans to kill all the Israelites! You must go to the king and save us!"

Esther came before the king, and he asked her, "What do you want?" She invited him to a dinner, asking for Haman to join them.

King Xerxes and Haman went to the dinner. Again the king said, "Tell me what you want. I will give it to you!" Queen Esther answered, "Please save my people, and my own life," she said. "Haman wants to kill all of us!"

The king became very angry with Haman and had him punished. He then made a new law to save all the people of Israel, including Queen Esther. Because Queen Esther spoke up to the king, the nation of Israel was saved.

Can you find your way through Esther's crown?

START

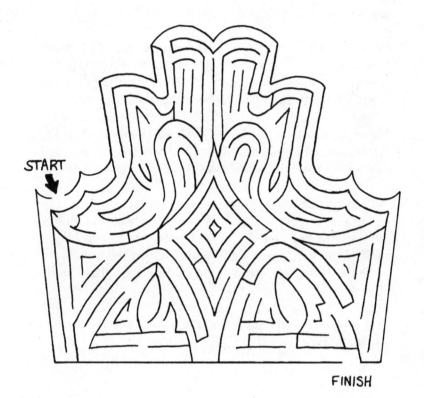

FINISH

Rebuilding the Walls of Jerusalem
Nehemiah

When the Babylonians attacked Israel and took the people away to become servants and slaves in Babylon, the soldiers destroyed the walls that surrounded the city of Jerusalem.

Seventy years later, God let the people of Israel become free again so they could return to their own country. However, when they arrived back in Jerusalem they saw a sad sight: The city walls had all been destroyed.

Nehemiah, a wise leader who loved God, went to King Artaxerxes of Persia and asked for help in rebuilding the city walls. King Artaxerxes was glad to help Nehemiah.

At first the people of Israel were discouraged. They thought it would be too hard to repair the walls. But Nehemiah did not give up. He got everyone to help. People took turns working on the wall and protecting the city from attackers. They finished building the whole wall in 52 days!

Can you find your way through the stones on the wall and get to the birds?

START

START

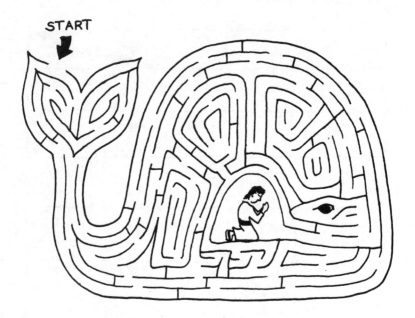

Jonah and the Great Fish
Jonah

The city of Nineveh was filled with wicked people. God was ready to destroy the city, but first he asked a prophet named Jonah to go warn the people in the city.

However, Jonah did not want to go to Nineveh. He did not care about the people there. So he tried to run away from God by going on a ship headed for a city named Tarshish.

While the ship was at sea, God sent a violent storm. The ship rocked so wildly that the sailors were afraid it would break up. They tried to pray to their gods for help, but the storm continued.

Jonah knew the storm was his fault because he had not obeyed God. He told the sailors, "Throw me into the sea, and the storm will go away."

When the men threw Jonah overboard, the sea became calm. Then God sent a great fish to swallow Jonah. Jonah was inside the fish for three days and three nights.

Jonah prayed to God, asking the Lord to help him. The fish then spit Jonah out upon the shore.

This time when God asked Jonah to go to Nineveh, Jonah obeyed. When the people of Nineveh heard about the warning from God, they turned away from their wickedness and followed the Lord!

Can you find your way to Jonah inside the belly of the great fish?

The Twelve Minor Prophets

The last twelve books of the Old Testament are all about prophets God sent to the people of Israel. These prophets spoke special messages from God to the Israelites.

Most of the messages were warnings from God, who wanted His people to turn away from their sin and follow Him.

The names of these twelve prophets are all on the next page. However, they are not in the correct order. With the help of the "ropes" in the maze, put the names in their proper order.

Micah

Nahum

Zephaniah

Haggai

Malachi

Habakkuk

Joel

Zechariah

Jonah

Hosea

Amos

Obadiah

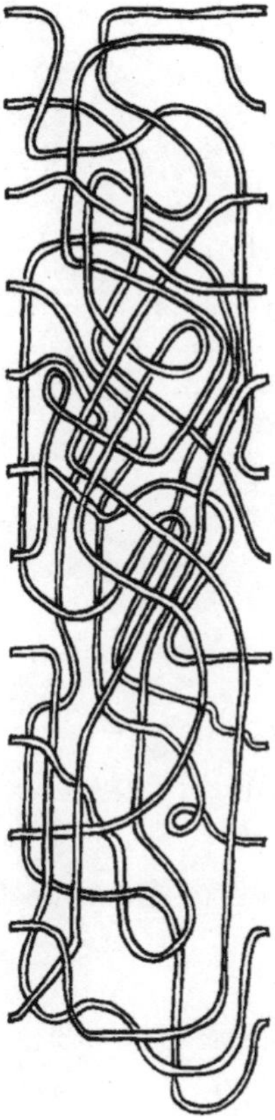

The New Testament

The New Testament

Here are the names of the books in the New Testament of the Bible. However, the letters are all mixed up! Can you spell the names of the books correctly?

thetMwa	1 ymthoTi
rMka	2 mTiyhto
ekLu	uiTst
nohJ	enomlihP
ctsA	srbeweH
nmasoR	Jsmae
1 rhniaoitCsn	1 erteP
2 ntCioanrhis	2 terPe
ntaialGsa	1 hoJh
Esnahsepin	2 ohnJ
inslpPiapih	3 nJoh
Cnolsaoiss	uedJ
1 naisahTsonels	levnoitRea
2 slenahisaTson	

Use this page to spell the book names correctly. If you need help, you can use your Bible.

_____   _____

_____   _____

_____   _____

_____   _____

_____   _____

_____   _____

_____   _____

_____   _____

_____   _____

_____   _____

_____   _____

_____

(The answers are on page 157 in the back of the book.)

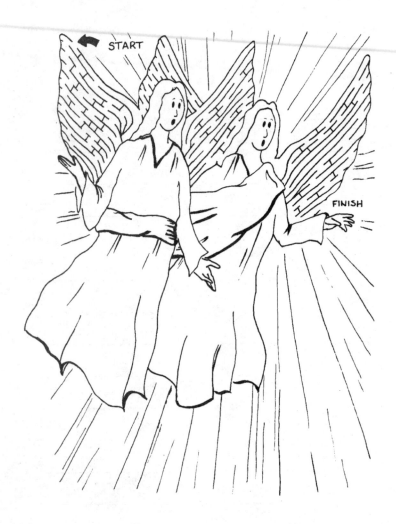

Good News of Great Joy
Luke 2:8-15

On a quiet, star-filled night, some shepherds were watching their sheep in the fields near the little town of Bethlehem. Suddenly an angel appeared, and the glory of the Lord shone brightly all around the shepherds. They had never seen anything like this before and were afraid.

"Do not be afraid," said the angel. "I have come to bring you good news of great joy. Today in the town of David a Savior has been born to you; He is Christ the Lord. You will find the baby wrapped in cloths and lying in a manger."

Then many angels appeared, and they praised God, saying, "Glory to God in the highest, and on earth peace to men on whom His favor rests."

When the angels had left, the shepherds looked at one another and said, "Let's go to Bethlehem to see the child that the angels told us about!"

Can you find your way through the maze? (Hint: You will need to go through the second angel's hair.)

Jesus Is Born!
Luke 2:16-20

The shepherds hurried to Bethlehem, and they found Mary, Joseph, and the baby. When they arrived, they told Mary about the wonderful message from the angels. Everyone was excited! Then the shepherds returned to their sheep, thrilled that they had seen the newborn Savior, Jesus Christ the Lord.

Can you find your way to the baby Jesus?

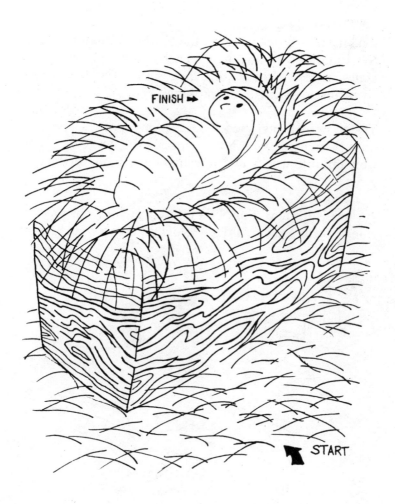

The Wise Men Visit Jesus
Matthew 2:1-12

One night, while looking at the sky, some wise men who lived in the east saw a new star. They knew it was a special star. "Let's follow it," they said. "That star is announcing the birth of a great king!"

The wise men prepared for their long journey and took with them some wonderful gifts for the new king. After traveling for weeks and months, they finally arrived in Jerusalem.

"Where is the new king?" they asked. Herod, who was the ruler over Jerusalem, did not know the answer. He became

afraid, because he did not want another king to replace him. Herod asked the Jewish leaders about it. They said, "This child was to be born in Bethlehem."

The wise men then followed the star to Joseph and Mary's house. They saw the young child Jesus with Mary and bowed down to worship Him. Then they gave the treasures they had brought for Him.

Can you help the wise men find their way to Bethlehem?

Jesus and John the Baptist
Matthew 3:1-17

In the wilderness of Judea was a special man named John the Baptist. God had chosen John to warn people about their sins and get them ready for Jesus' arrival.

"God wants you to turn away from doing what is wrong," said John the Baptist to everyone. "Turn away from your sin and follow God. Only He can help you do what is right." The people who accepted John's words were then baptized in the river.

When Jesus was ready to begin His ministry, He came to John the Baptist. John knew who Jesus was. Jesus went into the water, and John baptized Him. When Jesus rose up from the water, God's Spirit came down on Jesus like a dove. God said, "This is My Son; I am pleased with Him."

Starting at Jesus, can you find your way through the river to John the Baptist?

Fishers of Men
Mark 1:16-20

Jesus came to earth to help people know how they could become saved from their sins and become friends with God. He knew that someday He would return to heaven and that He needed to pick some special helpers (or disciples) to carry on His work.

One night, Jesus prayed to the Father about who He should pick. Afterward, Jesus went out and picked the men specially chosen by God. He went to the Sea of Galilee and saw Peter and Andrew. He said, "Come follow Me, and I will make you fishers of men."

What did Jesus mean when He said that? He planned to teach the disciples how to "catch" people and show them the way to heaven.

Can you find your way through the maze?

FINISH

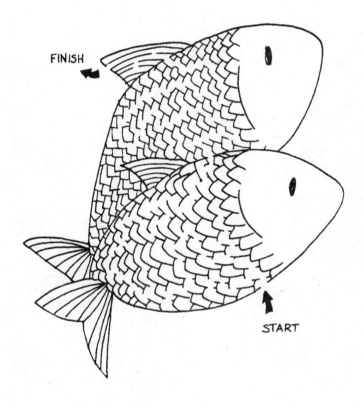

START

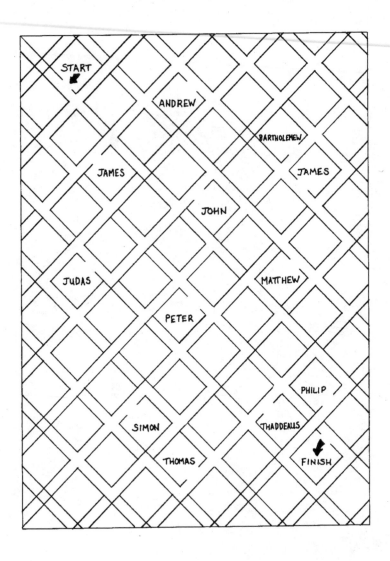

The Twelve Disciples
Matthew 10:1-4

Jesus chose 12 men to be His disciples. Each one was different, and each was chosen for a special reason. Their names were Peter, Andrew, James son of Zebedee, John, Philip, Bartholemew, Thomas, Matthew, James son of Alphaeus, Thaddaeus, Simon, and Judas.

Did you know that you, too, have been specially chosen by God? He has given you abilities that are different than everyone else's, and He has done that for a reason. You are special!

Beginning from the "Start" arrow, can you find your way to all 12 disciples, then go on to the "Finish" box?

The Story About the Farmer
Matthew 13:1-23

Jesus told His disciples and many other people a story about a farmer who planted seeds in his field.

"Some of the seeds fell on a path, and the birds ate them," said Jesus. "Some of the seeds fell on rocky soil, where they grew. But because their roots didn't grow deep, the hot sun scorched the plants. Other seeds fell among weeds, and were choked out. And still other seeds landed on good soil, where they grew up and became healthy plants bearing much fruit."

The disciples did not understand the hidden meaning behind the story. Jesus explained, "I am the farmer, who is spreading the message of the gospel. If a person's heart is hard, like the hardened pathway in the field, then he will not receive my message into his heart. Then there are people who think they want to follow Me. At first they say they accept Me, but later you can tell that their lives were not changed because they didn't bear any fruit. And last, those who receive My message in their heart and make it a part of their life will bear fruit—they will do many great things for Me."

Can you find your way from the "Start" arrow to the farmer's hand?

Jesus Stops a Storm
Matthew 8:18-27

What is happening here? The sea and the wind look very angry. Jesus and His disciples are in a horrible storm!

Jesus was asleep in the boat when the storm began. The disciples thought the storm would sink the boat. They were all afraid.

"Lord, save us! We're going to drown!" they shouted.

"Don't be afraid," said Jesus. "Trust in God." Then Jesus told the wind and the waves, "Be quiet!"

The disciples were amazed. They had never seen anyone who had power over nature. They knew Jesus had to be the Son of God.

Begin at the "Start" arrow and find your way to Jesus, who is standing in the front of the boat.

START

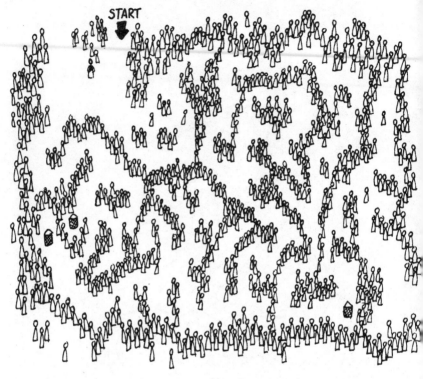

START

Jesus Feeds 5,000 People
Matthew 14:15-21

Jesus was so popular that large crowds followed Him everywhere. After one long day, the people were getting hungry. Jesus said, "Let's feed the people."

"But all we have are five loaves of bread and two fish," said the disciples. "Bring them to Me," said Jesus. He thanked God, then broke the loaves so the disciples could give the food to the people. When everyone was done eating, there were 12 baskets of food left over! Everyone was amazed at Jesus' miracle.

Jesus and the disciples are at the start of the maze. Help them go through the maze and collect all 12 baskets of food.

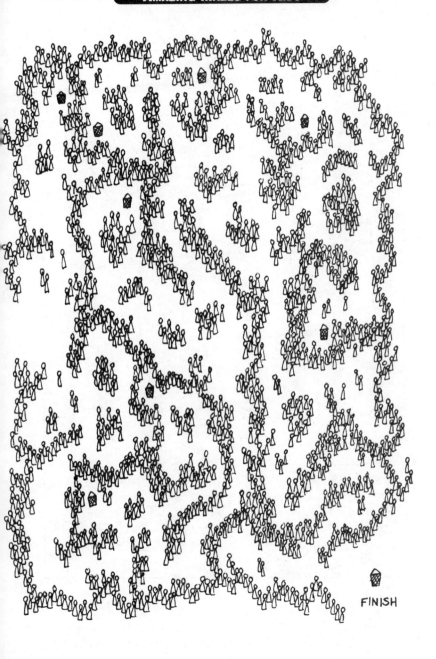

FINISH

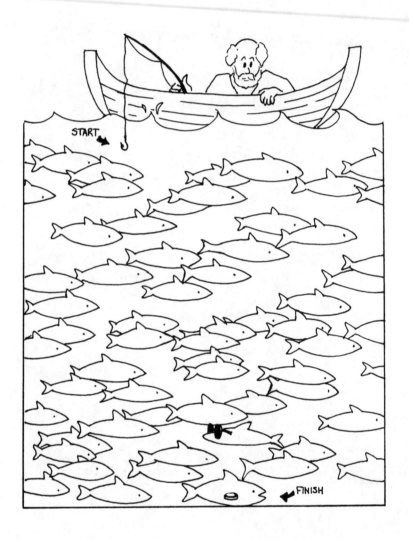

The Fish with the Coin
Matthew 17:24-27

When Jesus and His disciples traveled to the town of Capernaum, a tax collector came up to Peter and asked, "Does your teacher pay the temple tax?"

Peter answered, "Yes, He does." But Peter had no money, and didn't know how he should pay for the tax.

Jesus told Peter, "Go to the lake and throw out your line. Take the first fish you catch; in its mouth will be a coin. Use that to pay the temple tax."

How did Jesus know that the first fish Peter caught would have a coin in its mouth? Jesus knows everything because He is God. That means He knows everything that is happening to you each day! Aren't you glad He knows where you are and how to take care of you?

See if you can find your way from Peter's hook to the fish with the coin.

The Little Man in the Tree
Luke 19:2-10

Zacchaeus was a chief tax collector who lived in Jericho. He was very rich because he had taken lots of money from people unfairly.

One day Zacchaeus heard that Jesus was coming to Jericho. Zacchaeus wanted to see who Jesus was, but because he was so short, he could not see above the crowd. Then Zacchaeus had a great idea. He would climb a tree! Then he could see Jesus.

When Jesus walked by the tree, He looked up and said, "Zacchaeus, come down. I need to stay at your house."

Zacchaeus was very surprised! He could not believe someone good like Jesus would want to visit with him. Many of the people in the crowd were surprised, too. They asked, "Why is Jesus making friends with a man who cheats people out of their money?"

But Jesus helped to change Zacchaeus' heart. Zacchaeus said, "I will return the money I have taken unfairly, and will give to the poor."

Why was Jesus nice to a terrible sinner like Zacchaeus? Because He loved Zacchaeus and wanted to help him. In the same way, Jesus wants us to be kind to everyone around us.

Can you find your way through the tree? Start from Zacchaeus, and try to get down to the ground.

The Donkey Ride
John 12:12-19

Jesus and the disciples were about to go to Jerusalem to celebrate Passover, a special feast that remembered the time when God set the Israelites free from slavery in Egypt.

"Go into the village, and you will find a young donkey," Jesus told the disciples. When they returned with the donkey, Jesus rode it into Jerusalem.

Because Jesus was so popular, people began to wave branches and shout, "Jesus is our king! Hosanna! Hosanna!"

Everyone was happy, but little did they know that soon Jesus would be crucified on a cross. Only Jesus knew what was about to happen.

Begin from the "Start" arrow, and see if you can find your way through the palm branches to Jesus.

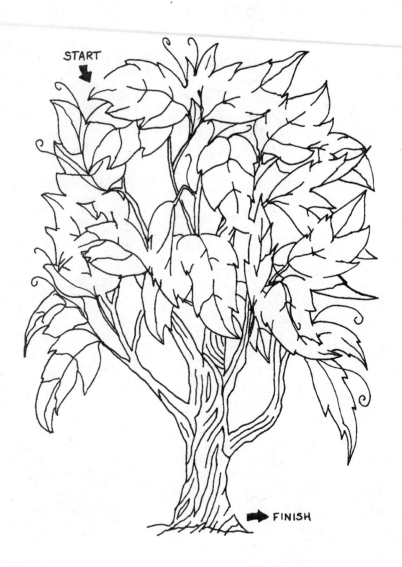

The Vine and the Branches
John 15:1-8

Before Jesus returned to heaven, He taught some important lessons to His disciples and everyone else who follows Him. One of these lessons was about the vine and the branches.

"I am the vine, and you are the branches," said Jesus. "As long as a branch is connected to the vine, it can bear fruit. In the same way, if you look to Me to give you life, strength, and wisdom, you will do well. But if you don't trust Me, then you will be like a branch that has been cut off from the vine. You will not be able to do anything in My power."

How can we, the branches, stay connected to Jesus, the vine? By trusting and believing in Him for everything, by talking to Him in prayer, and by learning about Him through the Bible.

Can you find your way from the branch (you) to the vine (Jesus)?

The Cross
John 18-19

There were some people in Israel—the religious teachers and leaders—who hated Jesus. For many years, they had taught the people of Israel that they had to work very hard to please God. They had to follow many laws if they wanted to get to heaven.

But Jesus said no; He said all people needed to do was to turn away from their sin, and God would forgive them.

Many people believed Jesus and followed Him because He spoke so wisely and did amazing miracles. "He has to be the Son of God," people said.

The religious leaders, however, did not agree. They wanted to kill Jesus. So they had Him arrested and accused Him of doing wrong. But Jesus had done nothing wrong. He was fully righteous.

The religious leaders had Jesus crucified on a cross. They thought that by killing Him, they could put an end to all that Jesus had done.

But they were wrong. Jesus knew He had to die on the cross. That was all a part of God's plan. The Bible says that sin must be punished, and everyone who is a sinner must die. Jesus, a perfect man without sin, died for us on the cross. He paid the punishment for sin so that we could be forgiven and made clean. He took away our sin and gave us His righteousness.

The day that Jesus died was a sad day, but Jesus knew His followers would not be sad for long!

Can you find your way up the hill to the cross?

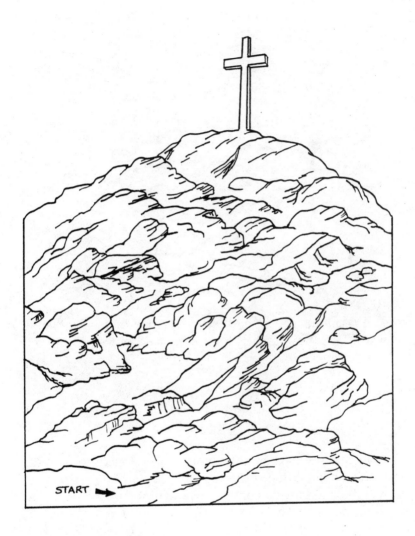

START ➤

START

He Is Risen!
Matthew 28:1-10

Early Sunday morning, the women who loved Jesus went to the tomb to bring spices to put on Jesus' body. Along the way, they asked each other, "Who will roll away the stone from the entrance so we can go into the tomb?"

When they arrived, they were surprised—the stone had already been rolled away! The tomb was empty. Jesus had risen! He was alive!

"Don't be afraid," said an angel at the tomb. "I know you are looking for Jesus. He is not here; He has risen just as He said He would. Go quickly and tell the disciples!"

Can you help the women find their way to the tomb?

Go Tell the World!
Matthew 28:19-20

Before Jesus went up to heaven, He met with the disciples up on a hill. "Go tell everyone the good news that I am alive," He said. "Go tell the world what I have taught you, and let everyone know how they can become saved."

Jesus' words were for us, too. He wants us to share with other people how they can become Christians!

Can you find your way to the different children of the world?

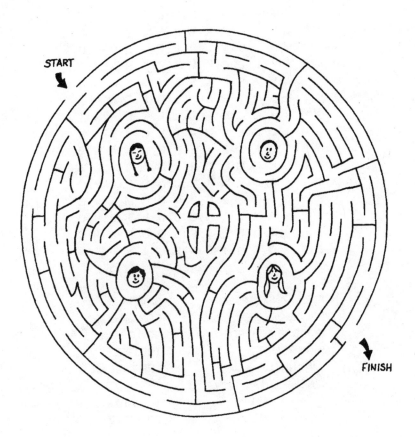

START

FINISH

```
T H E T R U T H R S T W L B Q J D
H S L N B R E A D O F L I F E K G
E Y Q D I F G W K Z R S G Y L I B
T I M M A N U E L P V Z H O U N D
R H G F I L C G R M D F T K X G C
U S O W U A P L J S O N O F G O D
E N O R S M T H S L E G F T W F Z
V G D N I B C N A W J F T E A K T
I A S C O O L S V A T L H N Y I H
N U H I Q F T Z I E N R E C A N E
E R E L N G M C O H A D W R H G W
M T P S R O L A R G C N O G L S O
R S H T L D W V N Z M D R M Y V R
T H E W A Y X R G C J U L I E N D
Q U R P T H E L I F E O D H K G C
J E D B Q S H I G H P R I E S T A
```

ALPHA AND OMEGA	SAVIOR
BREAD OF LIFE	SON OF GOD
GOOD SHEPHERD	SON OF MAN
HIGH PRIEST	THE LIFE
IMMANUEL	THE TRUE VINE
KING OF KINGS	THE TRUTH
LAMB OF GOD	THE WAY
LIGHT OF THE WORLD	THE WORD

(The answers are on page 158 in the back of the book.)

The Names of Jesus

One way we can learn more about Jesus is to know the names given to Him in the Bible. For example, we know that He is our shepherd because He is called the Good Shepherd. We also know that He is the Light of the world, and the King of kings.

In the book of Revelation, Jesus is called "the Alpha and Omega." *Alpha* is the first letter in the Greek alphabet, and *Omega* is the last letter. (These Greek words are used because the New Testament of the Bible was originally written in Greek.) So, when we call Jesus "the Alpha and Omega," we are saying that He is the first and the last. Jesus has been alive forever—He has no beginning, and He will have no end! Jesus is forever!

Because Jesus died on the cross for us, we too can live forever! Isn't that amazing?

See if you can find the names of Jesus in the word search puzzle.

Becoming a Christian
Acts 16:31

God sent Jesus to earth for a special reason: to die on the cross to pay for the punishment we deserved for our sins. In Romans 3:23, the Bible says everyone is a sinner. Because God cannot let sin into heaven, we need to get rid of the sin if we want to go to heaven. But that's impossible; we cannot remove the sin in our hearts.

Only Jesus can wash away our sin, because He is perfect, holy, and righteous. He came to take away our sin and give us His righteousness. Romans 6:23 says that the free gift of God is eternal life, which comes through Jesus Christ.

How can we become a Christian? By turning away from sin and asking Jesus into our heart. Then God will forgive us and save us, and make us into His children!

Have you received Jesus into your heart? If not, you can ask Him right now! If you want, perhaps your parents or your Sunday school teacher can help you pray to Jesus.

Acts 16:31 tells us how to become saved. Can you figure out what it says?

JESUS

YOU

THE

IN

LORD

BELIEVE

AND

BE

SAVED

WILL

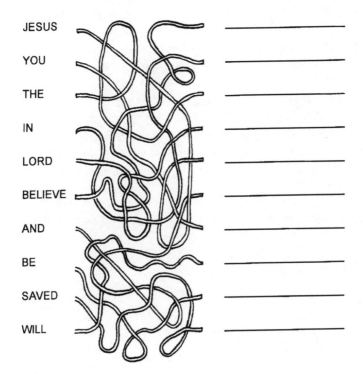

Paul's Journey to Rome
Acts 27-28

Paul was a bold man. He traveled to many towns and villages to tell people about Jesus. Paul also wrote several of the books that are in the New Testament of the Bible.

There were some people who did not like Paul. They didn't want him to share about Jesus. So they had him arrested. But that did not stop Paul! He also told the jail guards and other prisoners about Jesus!

Later, Paul was taken to Rome to go to court. While he was in Rome, he shared the good news about Jesus with many other people, including those who lived in the king's household!

Can you help Paul's ship find its way to Rome?

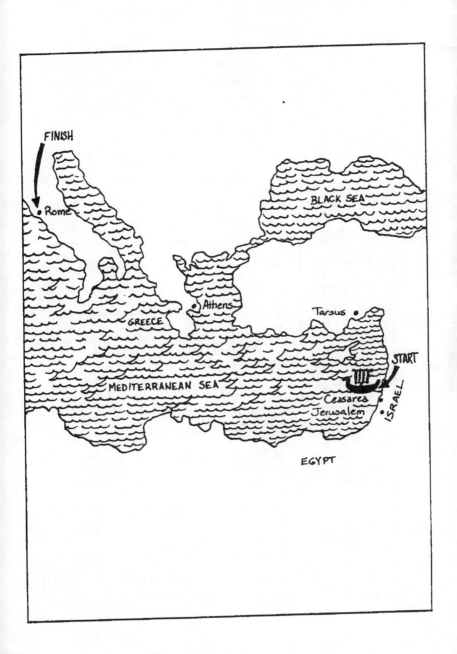

No temptation has seized you except what is common to man. And God is faithful; he will not let you be tempted beyond what you can bear. But when you are tempted, he will also provide a way out so that you can stand up under it.

—1 Corinthians 10:13

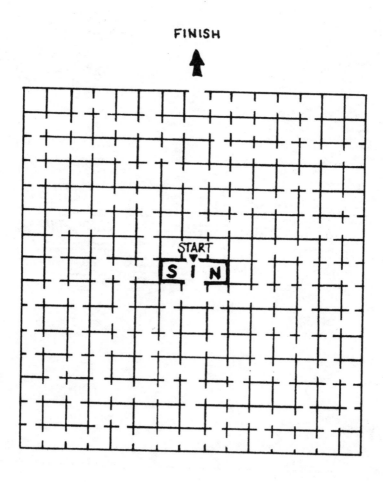

Escaping from Temptation
1 Corinthians 10:13

Do you know what temptation is? It's when you are thinking about doing something wrong. If you haven't done it yet, then you are being *tempted* to do something wrong. But if you go ahead and do it, then you have *sinned*.

Sometimes we are tempted to steal, lie, cheat, get angry, or hurt someone. When we start thinking about such things, what should we do? We should pray to God and tell Him we want to do what is right. He can give us the power to say no to temptation. The choice is up to us. Won't you choose God's way, and do what is right?

First Corinthians 10:13 is God's promise that He will help us say no to temptation and sin. If we look to Him for help, He will give us a "way of escape."

Start at the center of the maze where you see the word *sin*. Can you find your way of escape?

God's Kind of Love
1 Corinthians 13:4-7

How does God want us to love other people? The Bible tells us in 1 Corinthians 13:4-7: "Love is patient, love is kind. It does not envy, it does not boast, it is not proud. It is not rude, it is not self-seeking, it is not easily angered, it keeps no record of wrongs. Love does not delight in evil but rejoices with the truth. It always protects, always trusts, always hopes, always perseveres."

Won't you ask God to help you love other people this way?

Can you find your way through the maze to the word *love*?

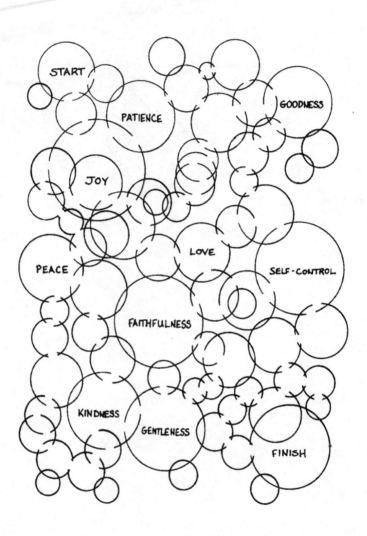

How Are Your Attitudes?
Galatians 5:22-23

Would you rather be around a joyful person or an angry person? Would you rather have a friend who is kind or who is mean?

It's always nice to be with a friend who is patient, good, and faithful. It hurts when someone is bad to us or breaks up a friendship.

How can we be the right kind of friend to other people, including our own brothers and sisters, and our parents? By having the right attitudes. God's Holy Spirit, who lives in the hearts of those who are Christians, can help us to have the right attitudes. These attitudes are listed for us in Galatians 5:22-23: "The fruit of the Spirit is love, joy, peace, patience, kindness, goodness, faithfulness, gentleness and self-control."

Do you know why these attitudes are called "the fruit of the Spirit"? Because the Holy Spirit helps to grow them in our hearts!

Can you find your way to all the fruit of the Spirit?

The Right Kinds of Thoughts
Philippians 4:8

In the last maze, we learned about the right kinds of attitudes. Do you know the best way to have those attitudes? By having the right kinds of thoughts!

Our thoughts affect the way we behave. If we have good thoughts, we will behave well. If we have bad thoughts, then we will act badly.

Philippians 4:8 tells us what kinds of thoughts we should have: "Whatever is true, whatever is noble, whatever is right, whatever is pure, whatever is lovely, whatever is admirable—if anything is excellent or praiseworthy—think about such things."

Can you find your way through the maze, and get to the words that describe what kinds of thoughts God wants us to have?

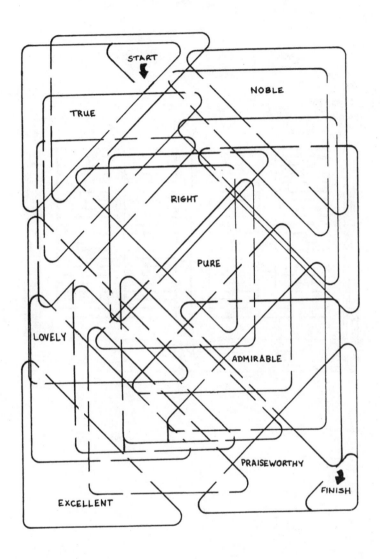

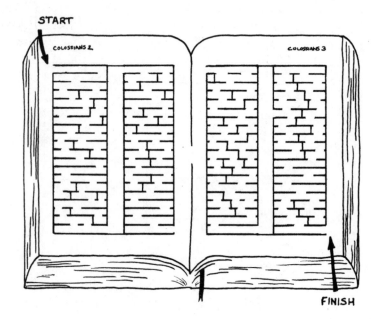

God's Word in Your Heart
Colossians 3:16

What is one way we can grow closer to God and become stronger in the Christian life? Memorize God's Word in our heart!

To *memorize* something means to repeat it in your mind again and again so that you'll never forget it. That's what Colossians 3:16 encourages us to do: "Let the word of Christ dwell in you richly." That means we are to let God's Word live in us richly.

When we memorize Bible verses, we will . . .

- know God better
- know His promises to us
- know the right way to live
- know how to treat other people

Also, when we memorize Bible verses, we can take them with us wherever we go! Then if we need help from God, we can remember what He says to us, even if we don't have our Bible with us.

Can you find your way through the maze on the Bible pages?

Praying and Giving Thanks
1 Thessalonians 5:17-18

What is prayer? It is talking to God and sharing with Him what is happening in your life. It's also a time for remembering His greatness, sharing your needs, and thanking Him for all that He has done for you.

First Thessalonians 5:17-18 tells us it is important to "pray continually; [and] give thanks in all circumstances."

Do you pray to God each day and thank Him for His good gifts to you? God loves to hear the prayers of His children!

Can you find your way through the maze?

START ⬇

FINISH

```
            G   T   L   R
            O   H   D   N
            F   I   W   L
            H   N   E   A
G   B   L   R   I   G   H   T   E   O   U   S
L   Q   E   M   S   S   A   B   L   I   B   M
M   E   R   C   Y   L   D   H   U   W   X   K
P   H   E   S   A   V   E   D   I   T   G   D
            K   U   L   C
            O   M   S   B
            L   U   H   E
            Y   S   G   C
            D   N   L   A
            I   O   L   U
            P   T   N   S
            R   L   F   E
            S   A   I   O
            P   J   T   F
```

HE SAVED	DONE
US NOT	BUT
BECAUSE OF	BECAUSE
RIGHTEOUS	OF HIS
THINGS	MERCY
WE HAD	

(The answers are on page 159 in the back of the book.)

Salvation: A Free Gift
Titus 3:5

Some people think they can get to heaven by doing good works. They say, "If I do enough good things, then I should be good enough to go to heaven."

But that's not what the Bible says. God tells us that we are all sinners, and no one can make it to heaven on their own. Only Jesus can save us. When He died on the cross, He made it possible to take our sin away and replace it with His righteousness.

Jesus loves us so much that He died so we could be in heaven with Him. He knew we couldn't save ourselves, so He gave up His life so that we can have life, too.

Isn't that the greatest kind of love?

Can you find the words to Titus 3:5 in the word search puzzle?

God's Promise to You
Hebrews 13:5

When you become a child of God, you are His child forever! Nothing can take you away from Him, and He will never leave you.

How do we know this? Because of the promise God gave to us in Hebrews 13:5. Can you put the words to Hebrews 13:5 in the right order, and figure out what the verse says?

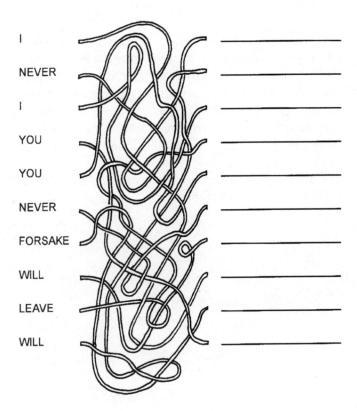

I   _____

NEVER   _____

I   _____

YOU   _____

YOU   _____

NEVER   _____

FORSAKE   _____

WILL   _____

LEAVE   _____

WILL   _____

Jesus Is Coming Again!
Revelation 21:12

Jesus is alive right now and living in heaven. If you are a Christian, He also lives in your heart.

But someday, Jesus will return to earth to set up a beautiful and perfect kingdom. He will wipe away everything that is bad, and He will be the best king that ever lived! Instead of a crown of thorns, which He wore on the cross, He will wear the crown of a king because He will be the King over all kings and Lord over all lords! And we will live with Him in His kingdom...forever! Isn't that exciting?

Can you unscramble the words on the following page, which are found in Revelation 21:12?

SOON!

COMING

AM

I

BEHOLD

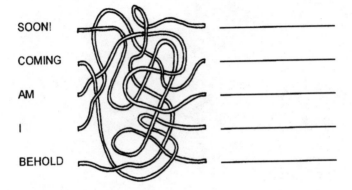

Puzzle Answers

The Old Testament
Pages 8-9

Genesis	Ecclesiastes
Exodus	Song of Songs
Leviticus	Isaiah
Numbers	Jeremiah
Deuteronomy	Lamentations
Joshua	Ezekiel
Judges	Daniel
Ruth	Hosea
1 Samuel	Joel
2 Samuel	Amos
1 Kings	Obadiah
2 Kings	Jonah
1 Chronicles	Micah
2 Chronicles	Nahum
Ezra	Habakkuk
Nehemiah	Zephaniah
Esther	Haggai
Job	Zechariah
Psalms	Malachi
Proverbs	

Job—Faithful to God
Pages 62-63

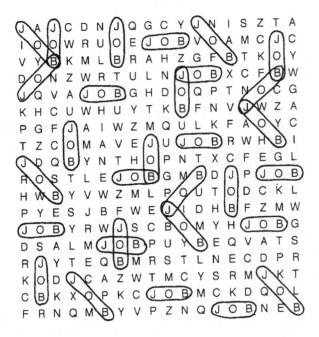

Job's name appears
in this word search 30 times!

God's Great Love
Pages 78-79

The New Testament
Pages 94-95

Matthew	1 Timothy
Mark	2 Timothy
Luke	Titus
John	Philemon
Acts	Hebrews
Romans	James
1 Corinthians	1 Peter
2 Corinthians	2 Peter
Galatians	1 John
Ephesians	2 John
Philippians	3 John
Colossians	Jude
1 Thessalonians	Revelation
2 Thessalonians	

The Names of Jesus
Pages 128-129

```
T H E T R U T H R S T W L B Q J D
H S L N B R E A D O F L I F E K G
E Y Q D I F G W K Z R S G Y L I B
T I M M A N U E L P V Z H O U N D
R H G F I L C G R M D F T K X G C
U S O W U A P L J S O N O F G O D
E N O R S M T H S L E G F T W F Z
V G D N I B C N A W J F T E A K T
I A S C O L S V A T L H N Y I H
N U H I Q F T Z I E N R E C A N E
E R E L N G M C O H A D W R H G W
M T P S R O L A R G C N O G L S O
R S H T L D W V N Z M D R M Y V R
T H E W A Y X R G C J U L I E N D
Q U R P T H E L I F E O D H K G C
J E D B Q S H I G H P R I E S T A
```

Salvation: A Free Gift
Pages 146-147

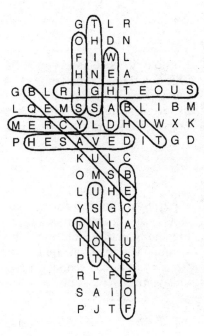

Also from
Steve and Becky Miller

MEMORY VERSE GAMES FOR KIDS
This entertaining book motivates kids to memorize God's Word with lively activities including secret code games, word searches, cryptograms, and crossword puzzles.

WORD SEARCHES FOR KIDS
Kids love word-search puzzles. Add them together with the Bible and you've got a winning combination! Terrific for family time, vacations, Sunday school classes—anytime kids want to have fun!

An Invitation to Write

If you would like to write to Steve and Becky Miller about *Memory Verse Games for Kids*, *Word Searches for Kids* or *Amazing Mazes for Kids*, you can write to them in care of:

Christian Family Bookshelf
P.O. Box 1011
Springfield, OR 97478-0201

Or call toll-free: 1-888-BOOK123
E-mail: srmbook123@aol.com